Treading Water

Chantal Wallace

／ BookLeaf
Publishing

India | USA | UK

Made with ❤ on the BookLeaf Publishing Platform
www.bookleafpub.in
www.bookleafpub.com

Dedication

To every version of myself that led me here. And to
those fighting their own battles with everything they've
got.

Preface

Art has always been a way to process feelings for me.
Poetry is one of my favorite mediums to work with.
Prose especially. I don't need to rhyme all the time,
sometimes I just want to get my point across in a way
that resonates. As I open up to share with the world, I
hope some of this resonates with you too.

Acknowledgements

I am incredibly grateful to my ancestors, family, and friends for all the support they have given me through every challenge and trial described in these pages. Thank you.

Interrupted

I may have been born and raised to love myself,
but the world snatched that love from me
during commercial breaks, between cartoons,
in the pages of magazines,
I was shown I wasn't enough by everything.

So i grew up,
moved out
fucked around and
found my own sense
of beauty
of shooting for the moon
of this wanderer ain't lost no more

Then I met you
and blind trust is a funny thing.
I let you peel back the layers
to see the scared parts of me,
but you were sneaky.

You took those
parts and
used them
to bend me

out of my mind
and into
your hands.

Then one day you just let go
I had dreams before you came along
I was whole before you came along
maybe I wandered to far
how do I find my way back?

Take up space

I may move through a world where deciding moment to
moment
if shrinking is the survival technique of the day.
But I don't need to shrink inside of me.
I don't believe in safe spaces,
but I believe in spaciousness.
And within me is enough room for every feeling.
The virtuous, the egregious, and the unclear.

My joy at seeing small creatures in massive trees.
My depression on full display in any mirror.
My contentment while rocking back and forth.
My rage at people being stolen away by the state.
My excitement at seeing old friends.
My fear for all of the Black girls missing.
My fulfillment while tending to the land.
My bitterness at being unheard, again.

But I am strong enough to hold
my gratitude and my grief,
my failure and my fruition,
my hell and my healing.

There is a universe within me.

I am infinite.

I am.

I am.

Consistency

One year from now,
you'll look back
one year from then
and whisper to yourself,
thank you,
thank you,
thank you.

I am still here
because you chose
to keep going.

One at a Time

I stepped on something sharp,
got stuck on something sticky,
tripped over something unseen,
and I fell,
and I fell,
until I couldn't fall any further.

I know I should watch where I'm going,
but I guess I have to be
eye level with my pain to even see it.

heavy sigh
I don't even know
how to begin
picking up the pieces.

R a g e

My anger is sacred.
I only give it willingly to those
who will recognize me through rage
and hold my truth with care.

They see my hurt, clear as quartz
and don't try to arrest my words.

They see my love, surrounded by pain
and don't try put out the flames.

How do I know you won't strange fruit me
in the depths of grief, wrapped in fire
because it's too hot for you to approach?

Why would I ever give you the chance to snuff me out?
My flame is eternal because I control the spark.
If you want smoke so bad,
learn to be uncomfortably warm.
Only then will I trust you to be my match.

H o l d   M e

I just want to be held.
I just want to be held.
I just want to be held.

Maybe if I say it enough times,
the words will stretch out wide
(Like the arms of my mother,
or the arms of a lover)
and swallow me into a cocoon.

Don't hold me back.
Don't hold me up.
Don't hold my words against me.
Just hold me.

Until I'm whole again,
and I can stand the rush of air.
Until my armor is back,
and I can stand tall without shaking.
Until I'm warm again,
and I don't need you to sustain me.

Please don't go.

I just want to be held.

i just want to be held.

Gifted

After learning the hard way
that love cannot be
earned or begged,
borrowed or bartered,
no matter how much
I work for it,
I was convinced
that I don't get to be loved
in this lifetime.

What a surprise it was to me
after doing nothing at all,
when you said, "I love you."

'We' are no longer 'us',
but love was still the most
amazing gift you ever gave me.

S p e l l s

I used to think magic wasn't real.
Just a collection of fancy petitions
candles, waters, feathers, herbs and concerns
stirred, burned, or whispered to.

But then I
heard a baby laugh at a sneeze,
watched a broken person rise whole from ash,
felt the ocean hold me and the weight of my grief,
smelled the forest as the sun peeked over the ridge,
tasted food that took me back in time.

And I don't really know what could be more magical
than that...

E a r t h

I love the feeling of dirt
crawling under my nails,
sliding between my fingers.

It reminds me of you,
Black, consuming, full-bodied,
and lovely in every way.

If you love me
as tightly as I hold onto this earth,
I trust you won't let me go.

Only nourish me
and watch me grow.

M o t h e r ' s   W o u n d s

My mother once told me it crushed her when my father
asked,
"why do you want to go everywhere with me?"
with enough sharpness to cut her heart out.
She whispered to me that she didn't get married
so she could continue to be alone.
She wanted to be with her love,
that didn't love her back.

So when you hold my hand
or touch me in the grocery store
as we take long walks up and down the aisles,
I feel sutures mending holes that aren't mine.
All the things you do for me
that draw deep gratitude from my gut
came from somewhere else first.
I was pulled from my mother's wound decades ago,
and I think I took some of her trauma with me.
It shaped the way I love.
The way I see love.
The way I give love away.
The ways I have worked for love
I could never have. It's excruciating.

I find romancé in the small things.
Intimacy in the mundane.
You touch my heart in all the ways
I never saw given to my mother.

Where Are You?

I exist
So someone like me must exist too
Someone unwrapped in complacency's untouch crying
into their already tear stained pillow

My love exists
So love like mine must exist too
Love that looks at you in the morning like
the beauty of the world is just beneath your eyelids
and they can't wait to see it again

My body exists
So a body like mine must exist too
Body bruised from so many mistakes,
yet still aching,
wondering what it feels like
to hold feeling loved inside of it

My eyes exist
So eyes like mine must exist too
Eyes that see pain in others
and hold gazes so they know
what it is to be seen without
having to hide behind cracked masks

My heart exists
So a heart like mine must exist too
Heart that is invested in healing generational trauma,
even though the history of those generations
was stolen from them

Where are you?
Where are you?
Where are you?

M a g i c i a n

I used to lay awake and dream of our montages.
Just us.
Sitting on the couch laughing together.
Waking up and seeing you sleeping peacefully next to
me.
Thinking disbeliefs.
Thinking only in nevers.

I never thought I'd have this.
I never thought I'd find you.
I never thought it'd hurt this much.
I never thought it'd feel this good.
I never wanted to let you go...

You're a magician.
You appeared out of nowhere
and stole my breath
without me even feeling it.

Barely Here

I don't think I have a poem in me today.
I've got a worn and weary body that I'm begging to keep
me upright. I've got hunger headaches and dehydration
to keep me company. I've got joints that crack louder
than that eggs I want to be scarfing down right now.
But I ain't got a poem.

I have depression. I'm six intrusive thoughts deep into
my evening. I have fears that have been beating on my
back door for weeks. I have enough tears to soak my
pillowcase that I wring out each morning. I have a
weight on my chest heavy enough to make me wanna
count down the days until I cave.
But a poem? Nah, I don't have that.

I got a to-do list that wraps around the block. I have 24
hours and it's never enough. I have enough side
occupations to preoccupy my every waking thought.
But I don't have no poem.

My words are so tired, I need spares just to finish this...

B e l o n g

I lay in bed,

I sleep,

I wake up,

I live,

on repeat,

with thoughts of you in between.

I find you in all the spaces.

Like sliding a book back into its place on a shelf.

It feels like

you always belonged here.

Stardust

How can you look at me
and let "love" fall out of your mouth?
I don't understand how you see my body,
skin pouring over itself and out of my clothes
and think beautiful.

You just see me and say,
"I see the vastness of the ocean,
the breadth of a sunrise on the horizon,
the *immensity* of the universe,
and marvel at its beauty.
Why would I see you any differently?
You're made of the exact same stardust."

Suncatcher

If every precious dawn
brought me closer to you,

I would chase the sun.

One More

Kissing you feels like fireworks.
Like stargazing and slow motion.
Feels like cotton candy melting in my mouth.
Like pizza parties and pretty balloons.
Like warm sand on a cool beach.

Kissing you feels like trying to lick the batter off every
inch of the beater.
Feels like holding my hands to my heart to catch the love
spilling out.
Like an active volcano about to erupt.
Feels like stimming, the slow rocking kind, the one that
makes sleep easy.
Like spinning around and around and around and
watching the world fly by.

Kissing you feels like a privilege.
Like a once-in-a-lifetime chance every time.
Like tingles when the blood comes back.
Feels like I love you's and you missed me's.
Like your lips can show me new worlds.
Like my lips were made for this luxury.

Can I have one more?

D r e a m i n g

As I lay my tired bones down and tuck my weary feet
beneath soft cotton sheets, my heart whispers,
I love you.
I hope you had the day you needed.
I hope you rest well tonight.
And as I close my eyes,
I hope I'll meet you in my dreams.

19. L i n e a g e s

They were free, so they sang.
They sang, so they could dance.
They danced, so they could pray.
They prayed, so they could heal.
They healed, so they could live.

And then they were taken.
Families destroyed.
Traditions broken.

They were enslaved, so they rebelled.
They rebelled, so they could run.
They ran, so they could march.
They marched, so I could live.
I live, so you can heal.

So go on my dear child, heal.

So they can pray,
And dance,
And sing,
And we can be free, together, once more.

Definition

Sun filters through window clings
painting rainbows on the ground like magic.
I step onto the warmest part of the rug
and watch you tend to sprouting green children
as gently as you tend to so many things since I've met
you.
You are free (enough), here.
Because at least in these four walls,
your body doesn't dictate your identity.
You do.
I love the person you are becoming.
And as you pick apart patriarchy
and assign your own definition to masculinity,
I find what femininity means to me.
I had never questioned it.
I had never picked apart
what it is to be a woman, to me.
I just lived out others norms.
Tried to prove I'm
Black and woman enough.
Black and graceful enough.
Black and beautiful enough.
Black and...

Who do I want to be?
Who do I say I am?

To Myself

O this body,
beautiful mahogany folds,
poured over ivory bones,
you are sacred.
The memories flowing
through your veins are ancient,
passed down from
the many who made you.

Remember the sounds
of their voices when they
come to you
in dreams,
in visions,
in whispers in the back of you mind.

They are guiding you.
Continually pushing,
always toward love,
forever toward liberation.